Design: Jill Coote
Recipes: D.M. Arnot, Ann Hohren, Rosie Brook,
Joan Davies, Chris Hardisty, Freda Hooter,
Pam Knutson, Vivien Margison, Alison Ray
Recipe Photography: Peter Barry
Recipe Styling: Bridgeen Deery and Helen Burdett
Jacket and Illustration Artwork: Jane Winton,
courtesy of Bernard Thornton Artists, London
Editorial: Laura Potts

CLB 3351
Published by Grange Books,
an imprint of Grange Books PLC,
The Grange, Grange Yard, London, SE1 3AG
© 1993 CLB Publishing,
Godalming, Surrey, England.
All rights reserved.
Printed and bound in Singapore
This edition reprinted in 1994
ISBN 1-85627-393-8

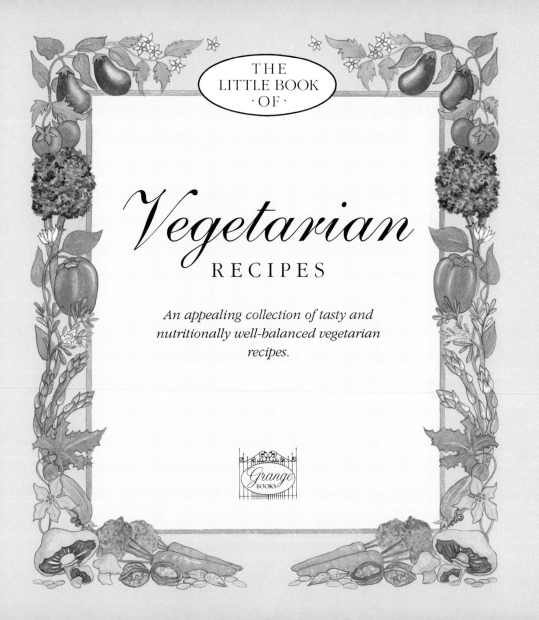

THE LITTLE BOOK ·OF·

Vegetarian

RECIPES

*An appealing collection of tasty and
nutritionally well-balanced vegetarian
recipes.*

Grange
BOOKS

Introduction

If you were to ask a cross-section of the population what they envisaged when they thought of vegetarian food, a large proportion would still describe it as bland and unimaginative, consisting of unappealing dishes made with lentils, and little else. Sadly this inaccurate image is one that has dogged vegetarian cuisine for many years, and appears hard to shake off. In truth, vegetarian cooking is neither bland nor unimaginative. At its very best, it is a subtle, tasty and innovative combination of textures and flavours. It uses ingredients that are often neglected in conventional cooking, such as beans, pulses, grains and nuts, and uses to full effect a wide range of fresh vegetables.

Vegetarianism has grown in popularity over the past few years. The reasons for this growth are varied. For many, the decision to have a meat-free diet is based on the belief that it is morally wrong to eat meat, while others choose to give it up as a protest against modern factory farming methods. A significant number, however, choose to adopt a vegetarian diet because they believe that it is better for their health. Today's diet, which is high in animal proteins, reflects the affluence of our society. Whereas our forefathers ate meat infrequently and in relatively small amounts, supplementing it with alternative forms of protein, like beans and pulses, we eat meat on a far more regular basis, and in larger quantities. It is thought that

the increase in consumption of cholesterol-rich animal proteins may play a part in the increased prevalence of coronary related diseases. This has led many people to cut down on their consumption of animal products, particularly red meat, which are known to be high in cholesterol.

Whatever one's diet, it is vital to ensure that the body gets all the essential proteins and minerals that it needs. Animal products, such as meat, fish, eggs and dairy goods conveniently provide all the amino acids – the building blocks from which proteins are formed – needed by the body. Vegetable proteins, while rich in amino acids, do not contain all of them. Different groups of vegetable proteins, such as grains, nuts and legumes (beans) contain different amino acids, so complementing each other. By combining different types of vegetable and dairy products it is possible to maintain the correct balance. A dish like Macaroni Cheese is a good example of how a non-meat dish can be put together to ensure the correct balance of protein.

You don't have to be a firmly committed vegetarian to enjoy vegetarian cookery, and these recipes are designed for the enjoyment of vegetarian and non-vegetarian alike. Using a wide variety of ingredients to create tasty, yet nutritionally well-balanced meals, they show just how versatile vegetarian cooking can be.

Wild Rice Soup

SERVES 4

A meal in itself when served with granary bread and a green salad.

PREPARATION: 15 mins
COOKING: 30 mins plus 40 mins for the rice

50g/2oz wild rice
420ml/¾ pint water
2 onions, chopped
1 tbsp unsalted butter
2 sticks celery, chopped
½ tsp dried thyme
½ tsp dried sage
850ml/1½ pints water or vegetable stock
2 tsps Vecon (vegetable extract)
1 tbsp soy sauce
6 small potatoes, peeled and roughly chopped
1 carrot, finely diced
Milk or single cream

1. Add the wild rice to the water, bring to the boil, reduce the heat and simmer for 40-50

Step 2 Sauté the onions in the butter until transparent.

Step 8 Add the milk or cream to thin the soup to the desired consistency.

minutes until the rice has puffed and most of the liquid has been absorbed.

2. Sauté the onions in the butter until transparent.

3. Add the celery, thyme and sage and cook for 5-10 minutes.

4. Add the water, Vecon, soy sauce and potatoes.

5. Simmer for 20 minutes or until the potatoes are cooked.

6. Blend the mixture in a liquidiser until smooth.

7. Return to the pan, add the carrot and wild rice.

8. Add the milk or cream to thin the soup to the desired consistency.

9. Reheat gently and serve.

Fennel and Walnut Soup

SERVES 4

A delicious soup perfect for special occasions.

PREPARATION: 15 mins
COOKING: 1 hr 10 mins

1 bulb chopped fennel
1 head chopped celery
1 large onion, chopped
1 tbsp olive or sunflower oil
75g/3oz walnuts, crushed
1150ml/2 pints vegetable stock
45ml/3 tbsps Pernod
140ml/¼ pint single cream
Salt and pepper
Parsley to garnish

Step 3
Liquidise the simmered ingredients together and return to the pan.

Slice the fennel bulb in half and then roughly chop.

1. Sauté the fennel, celery and onion in the oil over a low heat for ten to fifteen minutes.

2. Add the crushed walnuts and the stock and simmer for half an hour.

3. Liquidise the simmered ingredients together and return to the pan.

4. Add the Pernod, single cream and salt and pepper.

5. Reheat gently making sure that it does not boil. Serve garnished with parsley.

Cream of Carrot Soup

SERVES 4

A classic soup which is suitable for any occasion.

PREPARATION: 10 mins
COOKING: 35 mins

1 large onion, chopped
2 cloves garlic, crushed
1 tbsp olive oil
450g/1lb carrots, chopped
1 tsp mixed herbs
850ml/1½ pints vegetable stock
140ml/¼ pint soured cream
Salt and pepper

Step 2 Add the carrots, mixed herbs and stock.

Step 3 Bring to the boil and simmer for about 30 minutes until the carrots are soft.

1. Sauté the chopped onion and garlic in the oil until transparent.

2. Add the carrots, mixed herbs and stock.

3. Bring to the boil and simmer for about 30 minutes until the carrots are soft.

4. Cool a little and then liquidise until smooth.

5. Add the soured cream, season to taste and mix thoroughly.

6. Heat through gently, making sure the soup does not boil, and serve.

Watercress and Mushroom Pâté

SERVES 4

A delightful pâté served with thinly sliced brown bread.

PREPARATION: 10 mins
COOKING: 5 mins

25g/1oz butter
1 medium onion, finely chopped
75g/3oz dark, flat mushrooms, finely chopped
1 bunch watercress, finely chopped
100g/4oz low fat curd cheese
Few drops soy sauce
Scant ½ tsp caraway seeds
Black pepper

1. Melt the butter over a low heat and cook the onion until soft but not coloured.

Step 3 Put in the chopped watercress and stir for about 30 seconds until it becomes limp.

Step 7 Put into individual ramekin dishes or one large serving dish and chill for 2 hours.

2. Raise the heat, add the mushrooms and cook quickly for 2 minutes.

3. Put in the chopped watercress and stir for about 30 seconds until it becomes limp.

4. Place the contents of the pan in a blender together with the cheese and soy sauce.

5. Blend until smooth stirring the mixture if necessary.

6. Stir in the caraway seeds and pepper to taste.

7. Put into individual ramekin dishes or one large serving dish and chill for at least 2 hours until firm.

Red Lentil Soufflé

SERVES 4

Serve this tasty soufflé with watercress or salad.

PREPARATION: 15 mins
COOKING: 40 mins

100g/4oz red lentils
1 bay leaf
280ml/½ pint water
25g/1oz margarine or butter
75ml/2½ fl.oz double cream
2 egg yolks (size 3)
3 egg whites (size 3)
50g/2oz grated Cheddar cheese (optional)
Salt and pepper
Pinch of paprika

1. Pick over the lentils and remove any stones. Rinse well.

2. Place the lentils, bay leaf and water in a pan and bring to the boil.

Step 1 Pick over the lentils and remove any stones.

Step 6 Beat the egg whites until very stiff and fold into the mixture.

3. Simmer for 20 minutes or until the lentils are soft.

4. Remove the bay leaf and beat the lentils until they are very smooth.

5. Beat in the margarine, cream and egg yolks.

6. Beat the egg whites until very stiff and fold into the mixture.

7. Season and fold in the grated cheese.

8. Pour into a well greased soufflé dish and sprinkle with a little paprika.

9. Bake in a preheated oven 190°C/375°F/Gas Mark 5 for approximately 20 minutes or until the soufflé is well risen, firm and brown.

10. Serve immediately.

Mushrooms and Tofu in Garlic Butter

SERVES 4

A quick and delicious starter.

PREPARATION: 10 mins
COOKING: 12 mins

225g/8oz button mushrooms
2.5cm/1" root ginger
200g/8oz smoked tofu
100g/4oz butter
2 small cloves garlic, crushed
2 tbsps chopped parsley

---

1. Wipe the mushrooms with a damp cloth.

2. Peel and grate the root ringer.

3. Cut the smoked tofu into small 1.2cm/½" squares.

Step 2 Peel and grate the root ginger.

Step 7 Add the smoked tofu and heat through.

4. Melt the butter in a frying pan.

5. Add the crushed garlic and ginger and fry gently for two minutes.

6. Add the mushrooms and cook gently for 4-5 minutes until the mushrooms are softened.

7. Finally, add the smoked tofu and heat through.

8. Divide between 4 individually heated dishes, sprinkle with chopped parsley and serve at once with french bread or crusty wholemeal rolls.

Cauliflower and Broccoli Souflettes

SERVES 6
Serve as a winter-time starter or as a main meal with
rice salad and ratatouille.

PREPARATION: 15 mins
COOKING: 50 mins

350g/12oz cauliflower
350g/12oz broccoli
50g/2oz margarine
50g/2oz brown rice flour
420ml/¾ pint milk
50g/2oz Cheddar cheese, grated
1 large egg, separated
Good pinch of nutmeg

---

1. Break the cauliflower and broccoli into small florets and steam until just tender - about 7-10 minutes.

2. Melt the margarine, remove from the heat and gradually add the flour. Stir to a roux and

Step 1 Break the cauliflower and broccoli into small florets and steam until just tender.

Step 7 Divide the sauce evenly between the ramekin dishes.

add the milk gradually, blending well to ensure a smooth consistency.

3. Return the pan to the heat and stir until the sauce thickens and comes to the boil.

4. Cool a little and add the egg yolk and cheese, stir well and add nutmeg to taste.

5. Whip the egg white until stiff and fold carefully into the sauce.

6. Place the vegetables into 6 small buttered ramekin dishes and season.

7. Divide the sauce evenly between the dishes and bake immediately at 190°C/375°F/Gas Mark 5 for about 35 minutes until puffed and golden.

8. Serve at once.

Wheatberry Salad

SERVES 4

*This makes a substantial salad dish which provides an almost
perfect protein balance.*

PREPARATION: 20 mins

200g/8oz wheatberries, cooked
100g/4oz kidney beans, cooked
3 medium tomatoes, sliced
4 spring onions, chopped
2 sticks celery, chopped
1 tbsp pumpkin seeds

Dressing
4 tbsps olive or sunflower oil
2 tbsps red wine vinegar
1 clove garlic, crushed
1 tsp grated fresh ginger
1 tsp paprika
1 tbsp soy sauce
Fresh or dried oregano, to taste
Ground black pepper

---

1. Mix the salad ingredients together, reserving
a few pumpkin seeds and spring onions for
garnishing.

Step 1 Mix the salad ingredients together in a large bowl.

2. Shake the dressing ingredients together in a
screw-topped jar.

3. Pour over the salad and mix gently.

Step 3 Pour the pre-prepared dressing over the salad.

Sunset Salad

SERVES 4-6

Serve this colourful salad with cold nut roasts, raised pies or quiche.

3 dessert apples
350g/¾lb celery
4 medium mushrooms
75g/3oz walnuts
Lettuce leaves
75g/3oz alfalfa sprouts
75g/3oz black grapes

Dressing
125ml/4fl.oz mayonnaise
60ml/2fl.oz plain yogurt
Seasoning

Step 1 Cut the unpeeled apples into quarters and remove the core.

Step 6 Line a serving dish with well washed lettuce and spread the sprouts around the outer edge.

1. Cut the unpeeled apples into quarters and remove the core. Dice roughly.

2. Dice the celery and slice the mushrooms.

3. Chop the walnuts into quarters.

4. Mix the mayonnaise and yogurt together and season.

5. Put the apples, celery, mushrooms and walnuts into a bowl and fold in the dressing.

6. Line a serving dish with well washed lettuce and spread the sprouts around the outer edge.

7. Pile the salad in the centre and garnish with the grapes.

Carrot and Cashew Nut Roast

SERVES 6
A delicious roast to serve hot, but the full flavour is more prominent when the roast is served cold.

PREPARATION: 20 mins
COOKING: 1 hr 10 mins

1 medium onion, chopped
1-2 cloves garlic, crushed
1 tbsp olive or sunflower oil
450g/1lb carrots, cooked and mashed
225g/8oz cashew nuts, ground
100g/4oz wholewheat breadcrumbs
1 tbsp light tahini
1½ tsps caraway seeds
1 tsp yeast extract
Juice of ½ a lemon
65ml/2½fl.oz stock from the carrots or water
Salt and pepper

1. Fry the onion and garlic in the oil until soft.

2. Mix together with all the other ingredients and season to taste.

3. Place the mixture in a greased 900g/2lb loaf tin.

4. Cover with foil and bake at 180°C/350°F/ Gas Mark 4 for 1 hour.

Step 2 Mix the cooked onion and garlic with all the other ingredients.

5. Remove the foil and bake for a further 10 minutes.

6. Leave to stand in the baking tin for at least 10 minutes before turning out.

Step 3 Place the mixture in a greased 900g/2lb loaf tin.

Winter Crumble

SERVES 4-6

*A variety of hearty vegetables topped with oats and cheese
makes the perfect winter meal.*

PREPARATION: 20 mins
COOKING: 1 hr 5 mins

Topping
75g/3oz butter or margarine
100g/4oz wholewheat flour
50g/2oz rolled oats
100g/4oz Cheddar cheese, grated
¼ tsp salt

Filling
175ml/6fl.oz stock or water
280ml/½ pint sweet cider
1 tsp brown sugar
2 carrots, chopped
2 large parsnips, cut into rings
2 sticks celery, chopped
2 heads broccoli, cut into florets
¼ cauliflower, cut into florets
1 tbsps wholewheat flour
2 tbsps chopped parsley
1 medium onion, chopped and fried until
  golden
4 large tomatoes, skinned and chopped
225g/8oz cooked black-eyed beans

1. Make the topping by rubbing the butter into
the flour and oats until the mixture resembles
fine breadcrumbs. Stir in the cheese and salt.

Step 1 Rub the butter into the flour and oats until the mixture resembles fine breadcrumbs.

2. Mix the stock with the cider and sugar and
put into a large pan with the carrots and
parsnips.

3. Cook until just tender, remove the
vegetables and put aside.

4. Add the celery, broccoli and cauliflower to
the pan, cook until tender, remove and reserve.

5. Mix the flour with a little water, add to the
cider and cook until thickened, stirring all the
time. Add the parsley.

6. Place the onions, vegetables, tomatoes and
beans in a greased casserole and season well.
Pour the sauce over the mixture.

7. Sprinkle the topping over the top and press
down a little.

8. Cook at 200°C/400°F/Gas Mark 6 for 30-35
minutes or until the topping is golden brown.

Ratatouille Pie with Cheese and Peanut Pastry

SERVES 4-6

A colourful dish to make in the autumn when aubergines and courgettes are cheap and plentiful.

PREPARATION: 30 mins
COOKING: 1 hr

Ratatouille
2 tbsps olive oil
2 onions, finely chopped
4 tomatoes, skinned and chopped
1 aubergine, diced
3 courgettes, finely sliced
2 sticks celery, chopped

White sauce
50g/2oz flour
50g/2oz margarine
430ml/¾ pint milk

Pastry
50g/2oz butter
100g/4oz self raising flour
50g/2oz finely grated cheese
50g/2oz finely chopped salted peanuts
Milk
Beaten egg

1. Put the oil and all the vegetables into a large pan and cook gently for about 20 minutes or until soft.

Step 6 Place the pastry on top of the ratatouille mixture and trim the edges.

2. Melt the margarine in a separate pan and stir in the flour. Gradually add the milk and bring to boiling point stirring all the time.

3. Stir the sauce into the vegetable mixture and put into an ovenproof dish.

4. Rub the butter into the flour and add the cheese and peanuts.

5. Add a little milk and roll out the pastry.

6. Place on top of the ratatouille mixture, trim and brush with beaten egg.

7. Bake 190°C/375°F/Gas Mark 5 for about 30 minutes or until golden brown.

Quick Vegetable Chilli

SERVES 4

Serve this tasty chilli with wholemeal baps and salad.

PREPARATION: 15 mins
COOKING: 30 mins

2 large onions, sliced
1 tbsp olive oil
1 clove garlic, crushed
1 tsp chilli powder
400g/1 × 14oz tin tomatoes, chopped
400g/1 × 14oz tin of red kidney beans
1 small red pepper, chopped
1 medium courgette, sliced
½ small cauliflower
2 carrots, chopped
½ tbsp tomato purée
1 tsp dried, sweet basil
1 tsp oregano
¼-½ pint stock

1. Sauté the onions in the oil until soft.

2. Add the garlic and cook for 1 minute.

3. Add the chilli powder and cook for a further minute.

Step 3 Add the chilli powder and cook for a further minute.

4. Add the rest of the ingredients and simmer for 25-30 minutes.

5. Serve on a bed of brown rice.

Step 4 Add the rest of the ingredients and simmer for 25-30 minutes.

Tomato and Pepper Quiche

SERVES 4

Quiche is tastiest served with jacket potatoes and a crisp salad.

PREPARATION: 25 mins
COOKING: 55 mins

Pastry case
100g/4oz wholewheat flour
Pinch of salt
50g/2oz vegetable fat
A little cold water to mix

Filling
25g/1oz butter or margarine
1 onion, finely chopped
½ green pepper, finely sliced
½ red pepper, finely sliced
2 tomatoes, finely sliced
3 eggs
280ml/½ pint single cream
Seasoning
2 tbsps Parmesan cheese

1. Mix the flour and salt together.

2. Cut the fat into small pieces and rub into the flour until the mixture resembles fine breadcrumbs.

3. Add the water and mix until a ball of dough is formed.

4. Roll out to line a 20cm/8" flan tin or quiche dish.

Step 8 Arrange the onion and pepper on the bottom of the pastry case.

5. Prick the bottom lightly with a fork and cook at 180°C/350°F/Gas Mark 4 for 15 minutes.

6. Remove from the oven.

7. Meanwhile, melt the butter or margarine in a frying pan and sauté the onion and pepper until just softened.

8. Arrange the onion and pepper on the bottom of the pastry case followed by the sliced tomatoes.

9. Beat the eggs, and add the cream and seasoning.

10. Pour over the vegetables and sprinkle the cheese on top.

11. Return to the oven for 35-40 minutes until risen and golden brown on top.

Vegetarian Paella

SERVES 4-6

Perfect served with crusty bread and a green salad.

PREPARATION: 20 mins
COOKING: 45 mins

---

4 tbsps olive oil
1 large onion, chopped
2 cloves garlic, crushed
½ tsp paprika
350g/12oz long grain brown rice
1150ml/2 pints stock
175ml/6fl.oz dry white wine
1 × 400g/14oz tin tomatoes
1 tbsp tomato purée
½ tsp tarragon
1 tsp basil
1 tsp oregano
1 red pepper, roughly chopped
1 green pepper, roughly chopped
3 sticks celery, finely chopped
225g/8oz mushrooms, washed and sliced
50g/2oz mange tout, topped and tailed
100g/4oz frozen peas
50g/2oz cashew nut pieces
Salt and pepper

---

1. Heat the oil and fry the onion and garlic until soft.

2. Add the paprika and rice and continue to cook for 4-5 minutes until the rice is transparent. Stir occasionally.

Step 2 Add the paprika and rice and continue to cook for 4-5 minutes until the rice is transparent.

3. Add the stock, wine, tomatoes, tomato purée and herbs and simmer for 10-15 minutes.

4. Add the pepper, celery, mushrooms and mange tout and cook for another 30 minutes.

5. Add the peas, cashew nuts and seasoning to taste. Heat through.

6. Garnish with parsley, lemon wedges and olives.

Step 5 Add the peas, cashew nuts and seasoning to taste.

Millet Medley

SERVES 4

A tasty and wholesome recipe for the whole family.

PREPARATION: 10 mins
COOKING: 40 mins

1 medium onion, chopped
2 tbsps oil
225g/8oz millet
570ml/1 pint stock or water
Salt and pepper
75g/3oz cooked peas
75g/3oz sweetcorn
4 sticks celery, chopped
50g/2oz sunflower seeds
2 tbsps soy sauce

1. Sauté the onion in the oil for 2-3 minutes.

Step 3 Add the stock and seasoning, bring to the boil and simmer over a low heat for 30 minutes.

Step 6 Cook the sunflower seeds and soy sauce over a low heat until the seeds are dry.

2. Add the dry millet and cook for a few minutes, stirring all the time.

3. Add the stock and seasoning, bring to the boil and simmer over a low heat for 30 minutes.

4. Allow to cool.

5. Add the peas, sweetcorn and celery and mix well.

6. Place the sunflower seeds and soy sauce into a frying pan and cook over a medium heat, stirring continuously until the seeds are dry. Cool.

7. Just before serving, sprinkle with the toasted sunflower seeds.

Piper's Pie

SERVES 4

This attractive dish makes the perfect family meal.

PREPARATION: 20 mins
COOKING: 50-60 mins

450g/1lb potatoes, peeled and diced
175g/6oz mung beans
225g/8oz leeks
1 onion, sliced
½ tsp dill
2.5cm/1" fresh ginger, chopped or finely grated
1 tbsp concentrated apple juice
1 tsp miso

---

1. Boil the potatoes and mash with a little butter and seasoning.

2. In a separate pan, cover the mung beans with water and boil for 15-20 minutes until soft.

Step 3 Put the leeks, onions, dill, ginger and concentrated apple juice in a greased ovenproof dish.

Step 7 Cover the bean mixture with a layer of mashed potatoes.

3. Meanwhile, generously butter an ovenproof casserole dish and put in the leeks, onions, dill, ginger and concentrated apple juice. Mix well.

4. Drain the beans, reserving the stock, and add to the casserole dish.

5. Dissolve the miso in a little of the bean stock and mix into the casserole which should be moist but not too wet.

6. Cover and cook at 200°C/400°F/Gas Mark 6 for 30-45 minutes, stirring and adding a little more bean stock if necessary.

7. Remove from the oven and cover with a layer of mashed potatoes.

8. Return to the oven to brown or brown under the grill.

Fifteen Minute Goulash

SERVES 4

This quick and easy goulash is best served with baked potatoes.

PREPARATION: 10 mins
COOKING: 15 mins

1 onion, finely chopped
1 clove garlic, crushed
2 carrots, diced
3 medium courgettes, diced
2 tbsps olive oil
1 tbsp paprika
Pinch of nutmeg
1 heaped tsbp freshly chopped parsley
1 tbsp tomato purée
1 × 400g/14oz tin tomatoes
225g/8oz cooked red kidney beans or 1 × 14oz
    tin, drained and washed
225g/8oz cooked white kidney beans or 1 ×
    14oz tin, drained and washed
140ml/¼ pint tomato juice or stock
Salt and pepper
Soured cream or yogurt to serve

1. Put the onion, garlic, carrots and courgettes
into a pan with the olive oil and sauté for 5
minutes until softened.

2. Stir in the paprika, nutmeg, parsley and
tomato purée.

Step 1 Sauté the onion, garlic, carrots and courgettes for 5 minutes.

3. Add the rest of the ingredients except cream
or yogurt and cook over a low heat for 10
minutes.

4. Turn onto a hot serving dish and top with a
little soured cream or yogurt.

Step 4 Top the goulash with a little soured cream or yogurt.

Index

Cauliflower and Broccoli Souflettes, a tasty starter